Poems of Childhood

Poems of Childhood

Edited by Gail Harvey

AVENEL BOOKS
New York

First published in 1989 by Avenel Books, distributed by
Outlet Book Company, Inc., a Random House Company,
225 Park Avenue South, New York, New York 10003.
Manufactured in Singapore

Designed by Don Bender

Library of Congress Cataloging-in-Publication Data

Poems of childhood / edited by Gail Harvey.
        p.   cm.
    ISBN 0-517-69201-5
    1. English poetry.   2. American poetry.   3. Children—
Poetry.
I. Harvey, Gail.
PR1195.C47P58   1989
821.008'09282—dc20   89-34412
                                                  CIP

10   9   8   7   6   5   4

Contents

Introduction

Childhood is a magical time—an all too short period of innocence and wonder. For the adult, there is a fascination in observing the tiny, sleeping infant, the newly aware baby, the active, questioning toddler—and in seeing the "person" begin to emerge from the chrysalis of babyhood, as the child acquires greater independence, insight, and understanding.

Many of the world's great poets have written about childhood—of their enchantment with particular children, of experiences when they themselves were growing up, and of their own treasured memories of the pleasures, wonder, and even the pain of being a child. This new collection of notable poems of childhood includes such classics as Henry Wadsworth Longfellow's beguiling *The Children's Hour*, John Greenleaf Whittier's evocative *The Barefoot Boy*, and Alfred Tennyson's tender *Lullaby*. Here, too, you'll find Josiah Gilbert Holland's *Cradle Song*, which begins with the question every adult has at some time asked: "What is the little one thinking about?"

Mary Lamb writes of the difficulty in choosing just the right name for a newborn sister. In *Seven Times One* Jean Ingelow describes how grown-up a seven-year-old feels on her birthday. James Whitcomb Riley recalls the brightness and gaeity of his boyhood in *A Summer's Day*, and Elizabeth Barrett Browning recounts the adventurous joy of playing in a secret garden. In two sonnets from *Brother and Sister*, a sequence of eleven poems, the novelist George Eliot (the pseudonym of Mary Ann Evans) tells of her childhood relationship with her brother, Isaac Evans.

Included, too, is Henry Wadsworth Longfellow's *From My Armchair*, which he dedicated to the children of Cambridge, who presented to him, on his seventy-second birthday, a chair made from the wood of the village blacksmith's chestnut tree. (He had the poem printed, and gave a copy to each child who visited him and sat in the chair.)

This book is a celebration of childhood, and, like a pair of worn baby shoes, an outgrown sunbonnet, a threadbare, much-loved teddy bear, these poems are sure to reawaken warm memories and delight all who read and reread them.

GAIL HARVEY

NEW YORK
1989

INTRODUCTION TO
SONGS OF INNOCENCE

Piping down the valleys wild,
  Piping songs of pleasant glee,
On a cloud I saw a child,
  And he, laughing, said to me:

"Pipe a song about a lamb,"
  So I piped with merry cheer.
"Piper, pipe that song again."
  So I piped; he wept to hear.

"Drop thy pipe, thy happy pipe,
  Sing thy songs of happy cheer."
So I sung the same again,
  While he wept with joy to hear.

"Piper, sit thee down and write,
  In a book, that all may read."—
So he vanished from my sight,
  And I plucked a hollow reed;

And I made a rural pen;
  And I stained the water clear
And I wrote my happy songs
  Every child may joy to hear.

WILLIAM BLAKE

CRADLE SONG

Sleep, sleep, beauty bright,
Dreaming in the joys of night;
Sleep, sleep; in thy sleep
Little sorrows sit and weep.

Sweet babe, in thy face
Soft desires I can trace,
Secret joys and secret smiles,
Little pretty infant wiles.

As thy softest limbs I feel
Smiles as of the morning steal
O'er thy cheek, and o'er thy breast
Where thy little heart doth rest.

O the cunning wiles that creep
In thy little heart asleep!
When thy little heart doth wake,
Then the dreadful night shall break.

WILLIAM BLAKE

LULLABY

From *The Princess*

Sweet and low, sweet and low,
    Wind of the western sea,
Low, low, breathe and blow,
    Wind of the western sea!
Over the rolling waters go,
Come from the dying moon, and blow,
    Blow him again to me;
While my little one, while my pretty one, sleeps.

Sleep and rest, sleep and rest,
    Father will come to thee soon;
Rest, rest, on mother's breast,
    Father will come to thee soon;
Father will come to his babe in the nest,
Silver sails all out of the west
    Under the silver moon:
Sleep, my little one, sleep, my pretty one, sleep.

ALFRED TENNYSON

CRADLE SONG

From *Bitter-Sweet*

What is the little one thinking about?
Very wonderful things, no doubt;
  Unwritten history!
  Unfathomed mystery!
Yet he chuckles, and crows, and nods, and winks,
As if his head were as full of kinks
And curious riddles as any sphinx!
  Warped by colic, and wet by tears,
  Punctured by pins, and tortured by fears,
  Our little nephew will lose two years;
    And he'll never know
    Where the summers go;
He need not laugh, for he'll find it so.

Who can tell what a baby thinks?
Who can follow the gossamer links
  By which the manikin feels his way
Out from the shore of the great unknown,
Blind, and wailing, and alone,
  Into the light of day?
Out from the shore of the unknown sea,
Tossing in pitiful agony;
Of the unknown sea that reels and rolls,
Specked with the barks of little souls,—
Barks that were launched on the other side,
And slipped from heaven on an ebbing tide!
  What does he think of his mother's eyes?
What does he think of his mother's hair?
  What of the cradle-roof, that flies
Forward and backward through the air?

What does he think of his mother's breast,
Bare and beautiful, smooth and white,
Seeking it ever with fresh delight,
    Cup of his life, and couch of his rest?
What does he think when her quick embrace
Presses his hand and buries his face
Deep where the heart-throbs sink and swell,
With a tenderness she can never tell,
    Though she murmur the words
    Of all the birds,—
Words she has learned to murmur well?
    Now he thinks he'll go to sleep!
    I can see the shadow creep
    Over his eyes in soft eclipse,
    Over his brow and over his lips,
    Out to his little finger-tips!
    Softly sinking, down he goes!
    Down he goes! down he goes!
    See! he's hushed in sweet repose.

JOSIAH GILBERT HOLLAND

TO CHARLOTTE PULTENEY

*T*imely blossom, Infant fair,
Fondling of a happy pair,
Every morn and every night
Their solicitous delight,
Sleeping, waking, still at ease,
Pleasing, without skill to please;
Little gossip, blithe and hale,
Tattling many a broken tale,
Singing many a tuneless song,
Lavish of a heedless tongue;
Simple maiden, void of art,
Babbling out the very heart,
Yet abandoned to thy will,
Yet imagining no ill,
Yet too innocent to blush;
Like the linnet in the bush
To the mother-linnet's note
Moduling her slender throat;

Chirping forth thy petty joys,
Wanton in the change of toys,
Like the linnet green, in May
Flitting to each bloomy spray;
Wearied then and glad of rest,
Like the linnet in the nest;—
This thy present happy lot,
This in time will be forgot:
Other pleasures, other cares,
Ever busy Time prepares;
And thou shalt in thy daughter see,
This picture, once, resembled thee.

AMBROSE PHILIPS

CHOOSING A NAME

I have got a new-born sister;
I was nigh the first that kissed her.
When the nursing-woman brought her
To papa, his infant daughter,
How papa's dear eyes did glisten!—
She will shortly be to christen;
And papa has made the offer,
I shall have the naming of her.

Now I wonder what would please her,—
Charlotte, Julia, or Louisa?
Ann and Mary, they're too common;
Joan's too formal for a woman;
Jane's a prettier name beside;
But we had a Jane that died.
They would say, if 't was Rebecca,
That she was a little Quaker.
Edith's pretty, but that looks
Better in old English books;
Ellen's left off long ago;
Blanche is out of fashion now.
None that I have named as yet
Are so good as Margaret.
Emily is neat and fine;
What do you think of Caroline?
How I'm puzzled and perplexed
What to choose or think of next!
I am in a little fever
Lest the name that I should give her
Should disgrace her or defame her;—
I will leave papa to name her.

MARY LAMB

THE MOTHER'S HOPE

Is there, when the winds are singing
   In the happy summer time,—
When the raptured air is ringing
With Earth's music heavenward springing,
   Forest chirp, and village chime,—
Is there, of the sounds that float
Unsighingly, a single note
Half so sweet, and clear, and wild,
As the laughter of a child?

Listen! and be now delighted:
   Morn hath touched her golden strings;
Earth and Sky their vows have plighted;
Life and Light are reunited
   Amid countless carollings;
Yet, delicious as they are,
There's a sound that's sweeter far,—
One that makes the heart rejoice
More than all,—the human voice!

Organ finer, deeper, clearer,
   Though it be a stranger's tone,—
Than the winds or waters dearer,
More enchanting to the hearer,
   For it answereth to his own.
But, of all its witching words,
Those are sweetest, bubbling wild
Through the laughter of a child.

Harmonies from time-touched towers,
  Haunted strains from rivulets,
Hum of bees among the flowers,
Rustling leaves, and silver showers,—
  These, erelong, the ear forgets;
But in mine there is a sound
Ringing on the whole year round,—
Heart-deep laughter that I heard
Ere my child could speak a word.

Ah! 't was heard by ear far purer,
  Fondlier formed to catch the strain,—
Ear of one whose love is surer,—
Hers, the mother, the endurer
  Of the deepest share of pain;
Hers the deepest bliss to treasure
Memories of that cry of pleasure;
Hers to hoard, a lifetime after,
Echoes of that infant laughter.

'T is a mother's large affection
  Hears with a mysterious sense,—
Breathings that evade detection,
Whisper faint, and fine inflection,
  Thrill in her with power intense.
Childhood's honeyed words untaught
Hiveth she in loving thought,—
Tones that never thence depart;
For she listens—with her heart.

LAMAN BLANCHARD

A CHILD'S LAUGHTER

All the bells of heaven may ring,
All the birds of heaven may sing,
All the wells on earth may spring,
All the winds on earth may bring
    All sweet sounds together;
Sweeter far than all things heard,
Hand of harper, tone of bird,
Sound of woods at sundawn stirred,
Welling water's winsome word,
    Wind in warm wan weather,

One thing yet there is, that none
Hearing ere its chime be done
Knows not well the sweetest one
Heard of man beneath the sun,
    Hoped in heaven hereafter;
Soft and strong and loud and light—
Very sound of very light
Heard from morning's rosiest height—
When the soul of all delight
    Fills a child's clear laughter.

Golden bells of welcome rolled
Never forth such notes, nor told
Hours so blithe in tones so bold,
As the radiant mouth of gold
    Here that rings forth heaven.
If the golden-crested wren
Were a nightingale—why, then,
Something seen and heard of men
Might be half as sweet as when
    Laughs a child of seven.

ALGERNON CHARLES SWINBURNE

SEVEN TIMES ONE

There's no dew left on the daisies and clover,
　　There's no rain left in heaven.
I've said my "seven times" over and over,—
　　Seven times one are seven.

I am old,—so old I can write a letter;
　　My birthday lessons are done.
The lambs play always,—they know no better;
　　They are only one times one.

O Moon! in the night I have seen you sailing
　　And shining so round and low.
You were bright—ah, bright—but your light
　　　　is failing;
　　You are nothing now but a bow.

You Moon! have you done something wrong in
　　　　heaven,
　　That God has hidden your face?
I hope, if you have, you will soon be forgiven,
　　And shine again in your place.

O velvet Bee! you're a dusty fellow,—
    You've powdered your legs with gold.
O brave marsh Mary-buds, rich and yellow,
    Give me your money to hold!

O Columbine! open your folded wrapper,
    Where two twin turtle-doves dwell!
O Cuckoo-pint! toll me the purple clapper
    That hangs in your clear green bell!

And show me your nest, with the young ones in
        it,—
    I will not steal them away:
I am old! you may trust me, linnet, linnet!
    I am seven times one to-day.

JEAN INGELOW

I CANNOT CHOOSE

I cannot choose but think upon the time
When our two lives grew like two buds that kiss
At lightest thrill from the bee's swinging chime,
Because the one so near the other is.

He was the elder and a little man
Of forty inches, bound to show no dread,
And I the girl that puppy-like now ran,
Now lagged behind my brother's larger tread.

I held him wise, and when he talked to me
Of snakes and birds, and which God loved the best,
I thought his knowledge marked the boundary
Where men grew blind, though angels knew the rest.

If he said "Hush!" I tried to hold my breath;
Wherever he said "Come!" I stepped in faith.

GEORGE ELIOT

SCHOOL PARTED US

School parted us; we never found again
That childish world where our two spirits mingled
Like scents from varying roses that remain
One sweetness, nor can evermore be singled.

Yet the twin habit of that early time
Lingered for long about the heart and tongue:
We had been natives of one happy clime,
And its dear accent to our utterance clung,

Till the dire years whose awful name is Change
Had grasped our souls still yearning in divorce,
And pitiless shaped them in two forms that range
Two elements which sever their life's course.

But were another childhood-world my share,
I would be born a little sister there.

George Eliot

DAY DREAMS, OR TEN YEARS OLD

I measured myself by the wall in the garden;
The hollyhocks blossomed far over my head.
Oh, when I can touch with the tips of my fingers
The highest green bud, with its lining of red,

I shall not be a child any more, but a woman.
Dear hollyhock blossoms, how glad I shall be!
I wish they would hurry—the years that are coming,
And bring the bright days that I dream of to me!

Oh, when I am grown, I shall know all my lessons,
There's so much to learn when one's only just ten!—
I shall be very rich, very handsome, and stately,
And good, too,—of course,—'twill be easier then!

There'll be many to love me, and nothing to vex me,
No knots in my sewing; no crusts to my bread.
My days will go by like the days in a story,
The sweetest and gladdest that ever was read.

And then I shall come out some day to the garden
(For this little corner must always be mine);
I shall wear a white gown all embroidered with silver,
That trails in the grass with a rustle and shine.

And, meeting some child here at play in the sunshine,
With gracious hands laid on her head, I shall say,
"I measured myself by these hollyhock blossoms
When I was no taller than you, dear, one day!"

She will smile in my face as I stoop low to kiss her,
And—— Hark! they are calling me in to my tea!
O blossoms, I wish that the slow years would hurry!
When, when will they bring all I dream of to me?

Margaret Johnson

A BOY'S SONG

Where the pools are bright and deep,
Where the grey trout lies asleep,
Up the river and over the lea,
That's the way for Billy and me.

Where the blackbird sings the latest,
Where the hawthorn blooms the sweetest,
Where the nestlings chirp and flee,
That's the way for Billy and me.

Where the mowers mow the cleanest,
Where the hay lies thick and greenest,
There to track the homeward bee,
That's the way for Billy and me.

Where the hazel bank is steepest,
Where the shadow falls the deepest,
Where the clustering nuts fall free,
That's the way for Billy and me.

Why the boys should drive away
Little sweet maidens from the play,
Or love to banter and fight so well,
That's the thing I never could tell.

But this I know, I love to play
Through the meadow, among the hay;
Up the water and over the lea,
That's the way for Billy and me.

JAMES HOGG

JENNY KISSED ME

*J*enny kissed me when we met,
   Jumping from the chair she sat in.
Time, you thief! who love to get
   Sweets into your list, put that in.
Say I'm weary, say I'm sad;
   Say that health and wealth have missed me;
Say I'm growing old, but add—
                Jenny kissed me!

LEIGH HUNT

THE CHILDREN'S HOUR

Between the dark and the daylight,
 When the night is beginning to lower,
Comes a pause in the day's occupations,
 That is known as the children's hour.

I hear in the chamber above me
 The patter of little feet,
The sound of a door that is opened,
 And voices soft and sweet.

From my study I see in the lamplight,
 Descending the broad hall stair,
Grave Alice, and laughing Allegra,
 And Edith with golden hair.

A whisper, and then a silence:
   Yet I know by their merry eyes
They are plotting and planning together
   To take me by surprise.

A sudden rush from the stairway,
   A sudden raid from the hall!
By three doors left unguarded
   They enter my castle wall!

They climb up into my turret
   O'er the arms and back of my chair;
If I try to escape, they surround me;
   They seem to be everywhere.

They almost devour me with kisses,
   Their arms about me entwine,
Till I think of the Bishop of Bingen
   In his Mouse-Tower on the Rhine!

Do you think, O blue-eyed banditti,
   Because you have scaled the wall,
Such an old mustache as I am
   Is not a match for you all!

I have you fast in my fortress,
   And will not let you depart,
But put you down into the dungeon
   In the round-tower of my heart.

And there will I keep you forever,
   Yes, forever and a day.
Till the walls shall crumble to ruin,
   And moulder in dust away!

HENRY WADSWORTH LONGFELLOW

LITTLE BOY BLUE

The little toy dog is covered with dust,
 But sturdy and stanch he stands;
And the little toy soldier is red with rust,
 And his musket molds in his hands.
Time was when the little toy dog was new
 And the soldier was passing fair,
And that was the time when our Little Boy Blue
 Kissed them and put them there.

"Now, don't you go till I come," he said,
 "And don't you make any noise!"
So toddling off to his trundle-bed
 He dreamed of the pretty toys.
And as he was dreaming, an angel song
 Awakened our Little Boy Blue,—
Oh, the years are many, the years are long,
 But the little toy friends are true.

Ay, faithful to Little Boy Blue they stand,
 Each in the same old place,
Awaiting the touch of a little hand,
 The smile of a little face.
And they wonder, as waiting these long years through,
 In the dust of that little chair,
What has become of our Little Boy Blue
 Since he kissed them and put them there.

Eugene Field

WE ARE SEVEN

A simple child,
  That lightly draws its breath,
And feels its life in every limb,
  What should it know of death?

I met a little cottage girl:
  She was eight years old, she said;
Her hair was thick with many a curl
  That clustered round her head.

She had a rustic, woodland air,
  And she was wildly clad;
Her eyes were fair, and very fair;—
  Her beauty made me glad.

"Sisters and brothers, little maid,
  How many may you be?"
"How many? Seven in all," she said,
  And wondering looked at me.

"And where are they? I pray you tell."
  She answered, "Seven are we;
And two of us at Conway dwell,
  And two are gone to sea;

"Two of us in the churchyard lie,
    My sister and my brother;
And in the churchyard cottage I
    Dwell near them with my mother."

"You say that two at Conway dwell,
    And two are gone to sea,
Yet ye are seven! I pray you tell,
    Sweet maid, how this may be?"

Then did the little maid reply:
    "Seven boys and girls are we;
Two of us in the churchyard lie,
    Beneath the churchyard tree."

"You run about, my little maid,
    Your limbs they are alive;
If two are in the churchyard laid,
    Then ye are only five."

"Their graves are green, they may be seen,"
    The little maid replied,
"Twelve steps or more from my mother's door,
    And they are side by side.

"My stockings there I often knit,
    My kerchief there I hem;
And there upon the ground I sit—
    I sit and sing to them.

"And often after sunset, sir,
    When it is light and fair,
I take my little porringer,
    And eat my supper there.

"The first that died was little Jane;
    In bed she moaning lay,
Till God released her of her pain;
    And then she went away.

"So in the churchyard she was laid;
    And when the grass was dry,
Together round her grave we play'd,
    My brother John and I.

"And when the ground was white with snow,
    And I could run and slide,
My brother John was forced to go,
    And he lies by her side."

"How many are you, then," said I,
    "If they two are in Heaven?"
The little maiden did reply,
    "Oh, master, we are seven!"

"But they are dead—those two are dead,
    Their spirits are in Heaven!"
'Twas throwing words away, for still
The little maid would have her will,
    And said, "Nay, we are seven!"

WILLIAM WORDSWORTH

THE UNSEEN PLAYMATE

When children are playing alone on the green
In comes the playmate that never was seen.
When children are happy and lonely and good,
The Friend of the Children comes out of the wood.

Nobody heard him and nobody saw,
His is a picture you never could draw,
But he's sure to be present, abroad or at home,
When children are happy and playing alone.

He lies in the laurels, he runs on the grass,
He sings when you tinkle the musical glass;
Whene'er you are happy and cannot tell why,
The Friend of the Children is sure to be by!

He loves to be little, he hates to be big,
'Tis he that inhabits the caves that you dig;
'Tis he when you play with your soldiers of tin
That sides with the Frenchmen and never can win.

'Tis he, when at night you go off to your bed,
Bids you go to your sleep and not trouble your head;
For wherever they're lying, in cupboard or shelf,
'Tis he will take care of your playthings himself!

ROBERT LOUIS STEVENSON

UNDER MY WINDOW

Under my window, under my window,
  All in the Midsummer weather,
Three little girls with fluttering curls
  Flit to and fro together:—
There's Bell with her bonnet of satin sheen,
And Maud with her mantle of silver-green,
  And Kate with her scarlet feather.

Under my window, under my window,
  Leaning stealthily over,
Merry and clear, the voice I hear,
  Of each glad-hearted rover.
Ah! sly little Kate, she steals my roses;
And Maud and Bell twine wreaths and posies,
  As merry as bees in clover.

Under my window, under my window,
  In the blue Midsummer weather,
Stealing slow, on a hushed tiptoe,
  I catch them all together:—
Bell with her bonnet of satin sheen,
And Maud with her mantle of silver-green,
  And Kate with the scarlet feather.

Under my window, under my window,
  And off through the orchard closes;
While Maud she flouts, and Bell she pouts,
  They scamper and drop their posies;
But dear little Kate takes naught amiss,
And leaps in my arms with a loving kiss,
  And I give her all my roses.

THOMAS WESTWOOD

CHILDHOOD

In my poor mind it is most sweet to muse
Upon the days gone by: to act in thought
Past seasons o'er, and be again a child;
To sit in fancy on the turf-clad slope
Down which the child would roll; to pluck
    gay flowers,
Make posies in the sun, which the child's
    hand
(Childhood offended soon, soon reconciled.)
Would throw away, and straight take up
    again,
Then fling them to the winds, and o'er the
    lawn
Bound with so playful and so light a foot,
That the pressed daisy scarce declined her
    head.

CHARLES LAMB

PAST AND PRESENT

I remember, I remember
The house where I was born,
The little window where the sun
Came peeping in at morn;
He never came a wink too soon
Nor brought too long a day;
But now, I often wish the night
Had borne my breath away.

I remember, I remember
The roses, red and white,
The violets, and the lily-cups—
Those flowers made of light!
The lilacs where the robin built,
And where my brother set
The laburnum on his birthday,—
The tree is living yet!

I remember, I remember
Where I was used to swing,
And thought the air must rush as fresh
To swallows on the wing;
My spirit flew in feathers then
That is so heavy now,
And summer pools could hardly cool
The fever on my brow.

I remember, I remember
The fir trees dark and high;
I used to think their slender tops
Were close against the sky:
It was a childish ignorance,
But now 'tis little joy
To know I'm farther off from Heaven
Than when I was a boy.

THOMAS HOOD

THE DESERTED GARDEN

I mind me in the days departed,
How often underneath the sun
With childish bounds I used to run
    To a garden long deserted.

The beds and walks were vanished quite;
And wheresoe'er had struck the spade,
The greenest grasses Nature laid
    To sanctify her right.

   •   •   •   •   •

Adventurous joy it was for me!
I crept beneath the boughs and found
A circle smooth of mossy ground
    Beneath a poplar-tree.

Old garden rose-trees hedged it in,
Bedropt with roses white,
Well satisfied with dew and light,
    And careless to be seen.

.   .   .   .   .

To me upon my mossy seat,
Though never a dream the roses sent
Of science or love's compliment,
    I ween they smelt as sweet.

.   .   .   .   .

And gladdest hours for me did glide
In silence at the rose-tree wall,
A thrush made gladness musical
    Upon the other side.

.   .   .   .   .

Nor he nor I did e'er incline
To peck or pluck the blossoms white.
How should I know but roses might
    Lead lives as glad as mine?

My childhood from my life is parted,
My footstep from the moss which drew
Its fairy circle round: anew
    The garden is deserted.

Another thrush may there rehearse
The madrigals which sweetest are:
No more for me!—myself afar
    Do sing a sadder verse.

.   .   .   .   .

ELIZABETH BARRETT BROWNING

THE BAREFOOT BOY

Blessings on thee, little man,
Barefoot boy, with cheek of tan!
With thy turned-up pantaloons,
And thy merry whistled tunes;
With thy red lip, redder still
Kissed by strawberries on the hill;
With the sunshine on thy face,
Through thy torn brim's jaunty grace;
From my heart I give thee joy,—
I was once a barefoot boy!
Prince thou art,—the grown-up man
Only is republican.
Let the million-dollared ride!
Barefoot, trudging at his side,
Thou hast more than he can buy
In the reach of ear and eye,—
Outward sunshine, inward joy:
Blessings on thee, barefoot boy!

O for boyhood's painless play,
Sleep that wakes in laughing day,
Health that mocks the doctor's rules,
Knowledge never learned of schools,
Of the wild bee's morning chase,
Of the wild-flower's time and place,
Flight of fowl and habitude
Of the tenants of the wood;
How the tortoise bears his shell,
How the woodchuck digs his cell,
And the ground-mole sinks his well;
How the robin feeds her young,
How the oriole's nest is hung;
Where the whitest lilies blow,
Where the freshest berries grow,

Where the ground-nut trails its vine,
Where the wood-grape's clusters shine;
Of the black wasp's cunning way,
Mason of his walls of clay,
And the architectural plans
Of gray hornet artisans!—
For, eschewing books and tasks,
Nature answers all he asks;
Hand in hand with her he walks,
Face to face with her he talks,
Part and parcel of her joy,—
Blessings on the barefoot boy!

O for boyhood's time of June,
Crowding years in one brief moon,
When all things I heard or saw,
Me, their master, waited for.
I was rich in flowers and trees,
Humming-birds and honey-bees;
For my sport the squirrel played,
Plied the snouted mole his spade;
For my taste the blackberry cone
Purpled over hedge and stone;
Laughed the brook for my delight
Through the day and through the night,
Whispering at the garden wall,
Talked with me from fall to fall;

Mine the sand-rimmed pickerel pond,
Mine the walnut slopes beyond,
Mine, on bending orchard trees,
Apples of Hesperides!
Still as my horizon grew,
Larger grew my riches too;
All the world I saw or knew
Seemed a complex Chinese toy,
Fashioned for a barefoot boy!

O for festal dainties spread,
Like my bowl of milk and bread,—
Pewter spoon and bowl of wood,
On the door-stone, gray and rude!
O'er me, like a regal tent,
Cloudy-ribbed, the sunset bent,
Purple-curtained, fringed with gold,
Looped in many a wind-swung fold;
While for music came the play
Of the pied frogs' orchestra;
And, to light the noisy choir,
Lit the fly his lamp of fire.
I was monarch: pomp and joy
Waited on the barefoot boy!
Cheerily, then, my little man,
Live and laugh, as boyhood can!
Though the flinty slopes be hard,
Stubble-speared the new-mown sward,
Every morn shall lead thee through
Fresh baptisms of the dew;
Every evening from thy feet

Shall the cool wind kiss the heat:
All too soon these feet must hide
In the prison cells of pride,
Lose the freedom of the sod,
Like a colt's for work be shod,
Made to tread the mills of toil,
Up and down in ceaseless moil:
Happy if their track be found
Never on forbidden ground;
Happy if they sink not in
Quick and treacherous sands of sin.
Ah! that thou couldst know thy joy,
Ere it passes, barefoot boy!

JOHN GREENLEAF WHITTIER.

BOYHOOD

*A*h, then how sweetly closed those crowded days!
The minutes parting one by one like rays,
    That fade upon a summer's eve.
But O, what charm or magic numbers
Can give me back the gentle slumbers
    Those weary, happy days did leave?
When by my bed I saw my mother kneel,
    And with her blessing took her nightly kiss;
    Whatever Time destroys, he cannot this;—
E'en now that nameless kiss I feel.

WASHINGTON ALLSTON

THE OLD OAKEN BUCKET

*H*ow dear to my heart are the scenes of my childhood,
    When fond recollection presents them to view!
The orchard, the meadow, the deep tangled wildwood,
    And every loved spot which my infancy knew,
The wide-spreading pond and the mill that stood by it,
    The bridge and the rock where the cataract fell;
The cot of my father, the dairy house nigh it,
    And e'en the rude bucket that hung in the well.

That moss-covered bucket I hailed as a treasure,
    For often at noon, when returned from the field,
I found it the source of an exquisite pleasure,
    The purest and sweetest that nature can yield.
How ardent I seized it, with hands that were glowing,
    And quick to the white-pebbled bottom it fell.
Then soon, with the emblem of truth overflowing,
    And dripping with coolness, it rose from the well.

How sweet from the green, mossy brim to receive it,
　As, poised on the curb, it inclined to my lips!
Not a full, blushing goblet could tempt me to leave it,
　Tho' filled with the nectar that Jupiter sips.
And now, far removed from the loved habitation,
　The tear of regret will intrusively swell,
As fancy reverts to my father's plantation,
　And sighs for the bucket that hung in the well.

SAMUEL WOODWORTH

IN SCHOOL-DAYS

Still sits the school-house by the road,
    A ragged beggar sunning;
Around it still the sumachs grow,
    And blackberry-vines are running.

Within, the master's desk is seen,
    Deep scarred by raps official;
The warping floor, the battered seats,
    The jack-knife's carved initial;

The charcoal frescoes on its wall;
    Its door's worn sill, betraying
The feet that, creeping slow to school,
    Went storming out to playing!

Long years ago a winter sun
    Shone over it at setting;
Lit up its western window-panes,
    And low eaves' icy fretting.

It touched the tangled golden curls,
    And brown eyes full of grieving,
Of one who still her steps delay
    When all the school were leaving.

For near her stood the little boy
    Her childish favor singled;
His cap pulled low upon a face
    Where pride and shame were mingled.

Pushing with restless feet the snow
    To right and left, he lingered;—
As restlessly her tiny hands
    The blue-checked apron fingered.

He saw her lift her eyes; he felt
    The soft hand's light caressing,
And heard the tremble of her voice,
    As if a fault confessing.

"I'm sorry that I spelt the word:
    I hate to go above you,
Because,"—the brown eyes lower fell.—
    "Because, you see, I love you!"

Still memory to a gray-haired man
    That sweet child-face is showing.
Dear girl! the grasses on her grave
    Have forty years been growing!

He lives to learn, in life's hard school,
    How few who pass above him
Lament their triumph and his loss,
    Like her,—because they love him.

JOHN GREENLEAF WHITTIER

WOODMAN, SPARE THAT TREE

Woodman, spare that tree!
  Touch not a single bough!
In youth it sheltered me,
  And I'll protect it now.
T was my forefather's hand
  That placed it near his cot;
There, woodman, let it stand,
  Thy axe shall harm it not!

That old familiar tree,
  Whose glory and renown
Are spread o'er land and sea,
  And wouldst thou hew it down?
Woodman, forbear thy stroke!
  Cut not its earth-bound ties;
O, spare that aged oak,
  Now towering to the skies!

When but an idle boy
  I sought its grateful shade;
In all their gushing joy
  Here too my sisters played.
My mother kissed me here;
  My father pressed my hand—
Forgive this foolish tear,
  But let that old oak stand!

My heart-strings round thee cling,
  Close as thy bark, old friend!
Here shall the wild-bird sing,
  And still thy branches bend,
Old tree! the storm still brave!
  And, woodman, leave the spot;
While I've a hand to save,
  Thy axe shall hurt it not.

GEORGE P. MORRIS

MY EARLY HOME

*H*ere sparrows build upon the trees,
   And stock-dove hides her nest;
The leaves are winnowed by the breeze
   Into a calmer rest:
The blackcap's song was very sweet,
   That used the rose to kiss;
It made the paradise complete:
   My early home was this.

The redbreast from the sweetbrier bush
   Dropt down to pick the worm;
On the horse-chestnut sang the thrush,
   O'er the house where I was born;
The moonlight, like a shower of pearls,
   Fell o'er this "bower of bliss,"
And on the bench sat boys and girls:
   My early home was this.

The old house stooped just like a cave,
   Thatched o'er with mosses green;
Winter around the walls would rave,
   But all was calm within;
The trees are here all green agen,
   Here bees the flowers still kiss,
But flowers and trees seemed sweeter then:
   My early home was this.

JOHN CLARE

A SUMMER'S DAY

The Summer's put the idy in
  My head that I'm a boy again;
  And all around's so bright and gay
  I want to put my team away,
  And jest git out whare I can lay
  And soak my hide full of the day!
But work is work, and must be done—
Yit, as I work, I have my fun,
Jest fancyin' these furries here
Is childhood's paths onc't more so dear:—
And so I walk through medder-lands,
  And country lanes, and swampy trails
Whare long bullrushes bresh my hands;
  And, tilted on the ridered rails
  Of deadnin' fences, "Old Bob White"
  Whissels his name in high delight,
And whirrs away. I wunder still,
Whichever way a boy's feet will—
Whare trees has fell, with tangled tops
  Whare dead leaves shakes, I stop fer breth,
Heerin' the acorn as it drops—
  H'istin' my chin up still as deth,
And watchin' clos't, with upturned eyes,
The tree whare Mr. Squirrel tries
To hide hisse'f above the limb,
But lets his own tale tell on him.

I wunder on in deeper glooms—
  Git hungry, hearin' female cries
From old farm-houses, whare perfumes
  Of harvest dinners seems to rise
And ta'nt a feller, hart and brane,
With memories he can't explain.

I wunder through the underbresh,
   Whare pig-tracks, pintin' to'rds the crick
Is picked and printed in the fresh
   Black bottom-lands, like wimmern pick
Theyr pie-crusts with a fork, some way,
When bakin' fer camp-meetin' day.

I wunder on and on and on,
Tel my gray hair and beard is gone,
And ev'ry wrinkle on my brow
Is rubbed clean out and shaddered now
With curls as brown and fare and fine
As tenderls of the wild grape-vine
That ust to climb the highest tree
To keep the ripest ones fer me.
I wunder still, and here I am
Wadin' the ford below the dam—
The worter chucklin' round my knee
   At hornet-welt and bramble-scratch,
And me a-slippin' 'crost to see
   Ef Tyner's plums is ripe, and size
The old man's wortermelon-patch,
   With juicy mouth and drouthy eyes.

Then, after sich a day of mirth
And happiness as worlds is wurth—
   So tired that heaven seems nigh about,—
The sweetest tiredness on earth
   Is to git home and flatten out—
So tired you can't lay flat enough,
And sort o' wish that you could spred
Out like molasses on the bed,
And jest drip off the aidges in
The dreams that never comes again.

JAMES WHITCOMB RILEY

THE VILLAGE BLACKSMITH

Under a spreading chestnut-tree
　The village smithy stands;
The smith, a mighty man is he,
　With large and sinewy hands;
And the muscles of his brawny arms
　Are strong as iron bands.

His hair is crisp and black and long;
　His face is like the tan;
His brow is wet with honest sweat,—
　He earns whate'er he can;
And looks the whole world in the face,
　For he owes not any man.

Week in, week out, from morn till night,
　You can hear his bellows blow;
You can hear him swing his heavy sledge,
　With measured beat and slow,
Like sexton ringing the village bell,
　When the evening sun is low.

And children, coming home from school,
　　Look in at the open door;
They love to see the flaming forge,
　　And hear the bellows roar,
And catch the burning sparks that fly
　　Like chaff from a threshing-floor.

He goes on Sunday to the church,
　　And sits among his boys;
He hears the parson pray and preach,
　　He hears his daughter's voice,
Singing in the village choir,
　　And it makes his heart rejoice.

It sounds to him like her mother's voice,
　　Singing in Paradise!
He needs must think of her once more,
　　How in the grave she lies;
And with his hard, rough hand he wipes
　　A tear out of his eyes.

Toiling, rejoicing, sorrowing,
　　Onward through life he goes;
Each morning sees some task begin,
　　Each evening sees it close;
Something attempted, something done,
　　Has earned a night's repose.

Thanks, thanks to thee, my worthy friend,
　　For the lesson thou hast taught!
Thus at the flaming forge of life
　　Our fortunes must be wrought;
Thus on its sounding anvil shaped
　　Each burning deed and thought!

Henry Wadsworth Longfellow

FROM MY ARM-CHAIR

(To the Children of Cambridge who presented to me on my seventy-second birthday, February 27, 1879, this chair made from the wood of the village blacksmith's chestnut tree.)

Am I a king, that I should call my own
   This splendid ebon throne?
Or by what reason, or what right divine,
   Can I proclaim it mine?

Only, perhaps, by right divine of song
   It may to me belong;
Only because the spreading chestnut tree
   Of old was sung by me.

Well I remember it in all its prime,
   When in the summer-time
The affluent foliage of its branches made
   A cavern of cool shade.

There, by the blacksmith's forge, beside the street,
   Its blossoms white and sweet,
Enticed the bees, until it seemed alive,
   And murmured like a hive.

And when the winds of autumn, with a shout,
   Tossed its great arms about,
The shining chestnuts, bursting from the sheath,
   Dropped to the ground beneath.

And now some fragments of its branches bare,
    Shaped as a stately chair,
Have by my hearthstone found a home at last,
    And whisper of the past.

The Danish king could not in all his pride
    Repel the ocean tide,
But, seated in this chair, I can in rhyme
    Roll back the tide of Time.

I see again, as one in vision sees,
    The blossoms and the bees,
And hear the children's voices shout and call,
    And the brown chestnuts fall.

I see the smithy with its fires aglow,
    I hear the bellows blow,
And the shrill hammers on the anvil beat
    The iron white with heat!

And thus, dear children, have ye made for me
    This day a jubilee,
And to my more than threescore years and ten
    Brought back my youth again.

The heart hath its own memory, like the mind,
    And in it are enshrined
The precious keepsakes, into which is wrought
    The giver's loving thought.

Only your love and your remembrance could
    Give life to this dead wood,
And make these branches, leafless now so long,
    Blossom again in song.

HENRY WADSWORTH LONGFELLOW

MY PLAYMATE

The pines were dark on Ramoth hill,
    Their song was soft and low;
The blossoms in the sweet May wind
    Were falling like the snow.

The blossoms drifted at our feet,
    The orchard birds sang clear;
The sweetest and the saddest day
    It seemed of all the year.

For, more to me than birds or flowers,
    My playmate left her home,
And took with her the laughing spring,
    The music and the bloom.

She kissed the lips of kith and kin,
    She laid her hand in mine:
What more could ask the bashful boy
    Who fed her father's kine?

She left us in the bloom of May:
    The constant years told o'er
Their season with as sweet May morns,
    But she came back no more.

I walk, with noiseless feet, the round
    Of uneventful years;
Still o'er and o'er I sow the spring
    And reap the autumn ears.

She lives where all the golden year
    Her summer roses blow;
The dusky children of the sun
    Before her come and go.

There haply with her jeweled hands
    She smooths her silken gown,—
No more the homespun lap wherein
    I shook the walnuts down.

The wild grapes wait us by the brook,
    The brown nuts on the hill,
And still the May-day flowers make sweet
    The woods of Follymill.

The lilies blossom in the pond,
    The bird builds in the tree,
The dark pines sing on Ramoth hill
    The slow song of the sea.

I wonder if she thinks of them,
    And how the old time seems,—
If ever the pines of Ramoth wood
    Are sounding in her dreams.

I see her face, I hear her voice:
    Does she remember mine?
And what to her is now the boy
    Who fed her father's kine?

What cares she that the orioles build
    For other eyes than ours,—
That other hands with nuts are filled,
    And other laps with flowers?

O playmate in the golden time!
    Our mossy seat is green,
Its fringing violets blossom yet,
    The old trees o'er it lean.

The winds so sweet with birch and fern
    A sweeter memory blow;
And there in spring the veeries sing
    The song of long ago.

And still the pines of Ramoth wood
    Are moaning like the sea,—
The moaning of the sea of change
    Between myself and thee!

JOHN GREENLEAF WHITTIER

IT NEVER COMES AGAIN

*T*here are gains for all our losses,
    There are balms for all our pain,
But when youth, the dream, departs,
It takes something from our hearts,
    And it never comes again.

We are stronger, and are better,
    Under manhood's sterner reign;
Still we feel that something sweet
Followed youth, with flying feet,
    And will never come again.

Something beautiful is vanished,
    And we sigh for it in vain;
We behold it everywhere,
On the earth, and in the air,
    But it never comes again.

RICHARD HENRY STODDARD

*T*he children in the fields at play,
They pluck the flowers that grow;
We used to pluck the self-same flowers
'A many years ago.

We love to watch the children's game,
Their troubles and their joys,
For did we not the very same
When we were girls and boys.

ANONYMOUS